Journey Through a Thousand Thoughts

A book of poetry by

TaNaasha B. Herring

ISBN: 978-1-950861—50-7
Library of Congress Control Number: 2021921318

Printed in the United States of America
10 9 8 7 6 5 4 3 2 1

HIS GLORY

WENDELL, NORTH CAROLINA

INTRODUCTION

I don't really consider myself a writer or even a poet for that matter. I just know I've always been a thinker. I have been known to be quiet, pensive, and shy in my younger years, although I would not say so now. Then, somewhere around the age of eleven, I wrote my first poem: "If I was a Bird," it was called. Thankfully, I realized early on that I could be creative in putting my thoughts on paper, and the paper would be free of criticism or judgement. It would accept my thoughts and take them for what they are, without any need of explanation. Poetry has allowed me to tell stories and express thoughts while being as direct or discrete as I want. Most of my writing seems to come from a place of heaviness, and that is okay. Through the years, writing has proved to be therapeutic. Thus, I have generally written my best work in my worst moments.

Early on, I developed a love for writing. When I was in middle school, I remember I turned in a late English assignment. Later, the teacher called me to her desk and quietly explained that I should have had points deducted for turning in a late paper, but because it was so well written, she would not penalize me. English almost became my college minor.

My mother told me that when I was a toddler, some of the church choir members would almost embarrass themselves trying to get me to smile or react to their silly antics. But that serious little girl would barely crack a smile. In fact, it would probably surprise people to know that I saw a therapist in kindergarten. Why you ask? I remember going to see a guy in his office and he would ask me questions while I sat and played with Mr. Potato Head. As an adult, I asked my mother about that memory. She told me that I would not talk to anyone in kindergarten, so the school recommended I see a counselor. Funny, huh?

I've always been the serious type and have only more recently learned to laugh more, but to know me is to know this about me and to accept that my face is just my face.

To know me is to know that I'm not a woman of many words unless I have something to say. Even then, I'm selective about who I share my words with.

As a teen, I dreamed of one day publishing my poetry. This book is the realization of that dream.

TABLE OF CONTENTS

If I Was a Bird - my first poem

If I was a bird,
I would fly away,
Up in the sky, up with the rain.

If I was the sea,
I'd have lots of company
with all the fish that live in me.

If I was a frog,
I'd hop on a log,
Hippity hop, hoppity bog.

And If I was a human,
Of which I am,
I'd simply enjoy my beautiful land.

CHILDHOOD

Oh, Melancholic Child

Oh, Melancholic child, why do you cry?
I see your pain; you cannot lie.
I see the sadness in your eyes.

Oh, Melancholic child, why do you scream
And send aloud a silent plea.
Why won't you talk to me?

Oh, Melancholic child, why can't you say
Those things your heart keeps locked away
That only your eyes say?

Melancholic child I see, I see
The cry, the scream, the silent plea,
The secrets written with your eyes.
I know now what they mean,
For you, my child, are me!

Childhood

Return to me the innocence of a child
When life made sense, I rarely cried
Happiness was the only thing I cared to find,
When the only cares I carried for the day
Was to see how long I could stay out to play
When troubles seldom evoked or invaded my mind,
Joy was the only thing I ever cared to find

Return to me the innocence of a child
When nights were special cause dreams were sweet,
"Mommy" and "Daddy" tucked me in to sleep
The thought of tomorrow was nothing short of a treat
As I anxiously awaited another day,
I was allowed to be the child.
"Mommy" and "Daddy" were okay.

Return to me the innocence of a child
I thought that's what childhood ought to be
Did I do something wrong?
Or not enough, right?
Is it a privilege I lost?
Or did it ever belong to me?

Return to me the innocence of a child.
When life made sense 'cause I was a child
And that's all I had to be
Never worried about growing up before my time,
Maybe it's just an illusion in my mind
Or…maybe it's a lie they tell us all

And "childhood" doesn't really exist at all.

Return to me the innocence of a child

Daddy's Little Girl

Every little girl dreams of becoming the 'apple of his eye',
To be able to call him "Daddy" so purely and innocently.
And know he'll answer with a loving reply,
To know that he is "Daddy" and truly wants to be,
He'll care for her and strive
To love her unconditionally.
To know he'll always be there
As she grows into a woman of grace and purpose,
And if she somehow loses her way,
He'll help her regain focus.
She looks to lean on him to show her loves pure way
And trust that he will be her 'knight in shining armor,'
No, not perfect- but a man of integrity and honor,
Who perhaps will one day give her away
To a man as good, or even better than he.

They say little girls grow up to marry a man just like their dad,
But what picture do they follow when they've not had
The example to show the way?
Yes, many a girl has turned out just fine anyway.
If you're a little girl,
And Daddy is not around,
Don't let that dampen your spirit.
Don't let that keep you down.
Don't keep looking for someone who perhaps doesn't want to be found.
Don't blame yourself for needing something he cannot give.
Don't worry; you'll find your way, eventually -I did.

No, not all of us get to be daddy's little girl.
Perhaps it's God's protection.
It could be worse; he could be there, not desiring to be
Though not God's plan, things sometimes happen
For reasons we cannot see.
And we cannot blame ourselves
For the love we missed.
Eventually, God's purpose will manifest.
Yes, trust that He does know best.
And when you still have more questions than answers,
It's okay to wonder "why,"
But remember to give yourself grace
And keep your head held high.

You may not be "Daddy's little girl"
But you have a Father in heaven
Who loves you more than any man ever can
That matters more.

LISTEN!

Young girl dressed in blue
Angry face, brown hair, and eyes,
"Someone, please listen to me," she cries,
"Don't you hear me talking?
My anger knots inside my throat as tears run from my eyes.
I cannot breathe.
Someone, please listen to me.
This anger of mine fires like fierce bullets aimed at cement walls.
Its impact sounds like silent explosions.
Black smoke is left in its path.
"Let me out," she cries.
The smoke of her anger makes her afraid
So she stands still inside her pain
"But still I cannot breathe-
- if only you had listened to me!"

Father in God

Growing up without a father,
There was always a hole deep within.
At times, the hole was filled with despair,
But 'God doesn't give you more than you can bear.'
So, there must be a reason for this emptiness.

I would often cry out and still do cry,
"Why don't I have a dad?"
But how could I miss what I've never had?
Indeed, I don't miss the feeling of rejection.
The heart knows when something's been missing.

I've always been looking,
Searching and praying,
To find those things worth holding onto,
Those things that could maybe fill my hole.
And I'm learning that there's only One who can heal my soul.

Now that older I am becoming
The hole has filled itself from time to time
With worthless things like
unfulfilling love, envy, and anger;
Things that do not satisfy.

Often, I feel the need to plead with God,
To send His comfort and grace.
With tears streaming down my face,
God sends His peace
And reassures me along the way that He can make me whole.

Moment by moment, He holds me, and I know!

This void I have is slowly being filled.
God is my Father, and only He heals.
I know from just how far I've come.
No one can tell me God is not real.
And though I may cry in my darkest nights, my God dries my eyes.
Yes! He is *more* than a Father to me.

TEARS

TEARS

TEARS

Do my tears touch heaven?
I try so hard to stop them.
But they just keep flowing.
I cannot stop them.
I do not understand it.
They flow from my eyes,
Trickle-down my cheeks,
And collect on my pillow.
They flow . . .
          And flow . . .
                    And flow . . .
My heart races.
My chest pounds.
I long for someone to hold me until I am content
And tell me it will be ok.
But there is no one.
Can heaven feel my tears?

CAPTIVITY

I'm hurting
And nobody knows
I feel this pain deep down inside,
I wonder why
I thought I had grown, matured, advanced
And the tears would no longer make my emotions dance
To the rhythm of sadness and blues
I thought I could be happy if I choose
But I do choose happiness
Maybe it's a test to see if my emotions work
But they always have
Strong and passionate-
They hold me captive to myself,
Rob me of the peace that I long for within
And leave me with nothing to hold onto
-I'm hurting! And nobody knows

HELLO?

Hello?
Does anybody see me?
Does anyone hear me?
Is anybody there?

There's a stranger in this house and perhaps it is me.
Hello! Do you even care?

My words go unheard, my tears unseen.
You seem to notice when I scream.
Yet, you do not listen.
So, tell me, what am I missing?

If I compete with the chaos or if I'm swallowed in the storm,
The result is the same.
So again, the questions remain.

Hello?
Why don't you see me?
Why don't you hear me?
Why don't you care?

Bruised!

Bruised
That's what I am
That's how I feel
My heart's been hurt; many tears I cry have yet to heal

Bruised
Can't remember the beginning
Can't see an end
But I pray my soul to God, that this isn't how it ends

Bruised
Yes, redundant I sound
But I can't say it enough; in my own tears, I drown
My heart aches like it's been wrung between two angry hands
Dealing with pain that's hard to understand
I pray I find control before it takes control of me
But I know there are no guarantees, so for now, I remain

Bruised,
Praying that time will heal
And maybe I'll become that person, not afraid again to feel
As I heal from the scars that have left a bruise
I pray that my sanity I will not lose
And that, after a time, I will no longer be
Bruised

LIFE

CHANGE

The one thing that's constant
Never stands still
Yet, everyone fights it tooth and nail
As if we all expect the world to keep spinning while time itself stands still,
We all wish we could advance
And become better with time
But time leaves us in the dust
As we think with yesterday's minds

The day is a new one
Having the same sun but a different light
Yet, our minds are still the same
Thinking the thoughts of yesterday

With one hand outstretched to the future
And the other holding onto the past
Preventing us from living in the present
We're blinded by the reality of what isn't,
And struggle to see that it is we
Who hold ourselves back
By fearing this thing that will always be
This truth is strange
The one thing that's constant
Is
CHANGE

The Game

(Written in 1999)

Brought into the world
Innocent she came
Lived each day
Without knowing the name of the game.
Had to find the way,
And so she tried,
Without any idea
Of what she'd find.

The game was played,
The rules violated.
Soon she knew
That she had been perpetrated
Left confused,
Torn and abused,
She refused.
Her mouth remained shut
Yet they knew.

More frequent
Became the attacks
It was now her go
She didn't like this game, you know.
She made her move
And then was done
The turn was switched
The damage done.

But then she learned
Through each play
The rules changed,
Little variations here and there,
Never the same
She always knew what came next
Never wanted to guess

Couldn't run
Nowhere to hide
She crawled up in a hole and died.
Or did she?
Nearly
She had to define the word unique
Everything seemed so dark and bleak
Was the game finally over?
No sooner than she thought
Had there started another

****

PART II

Word had gotten out
She just couldn't
Either way, she was dying
Had she said or had she not.

Nothing to do
So, she lay to think
Soon found herself fast asleep
On the floor,

The thought of being loved
By anything, anyone was appeasing.
She lay
Cold but warm
Reaching out for the empty embrace.

She was running – clandestinely
In search of a better life
Permanent scars invade her
Yet would never be seen
Far too deep to understand what they mean.

The road was dark and narrow
She began to freeze
But she kept running; she refused to stop. She had to go on
There had to be a better way.

Back on the floor, she lay
Dreaming it all away,
But it wasn't
Reality was still there.
Who would've ever known
The cold could be so warm?

She had to stay out of the way
She had done her worst by saying
She wanted it all to go away…
Her hunger and thirst
It should not have been
But who would've known?

What it did to her then.

She survived
But was it over?

A Leap of Faith

Been here before
It's not all new
Pondering the dilemma of what to do
Choices to make
Weighing the stakes
The pros and the cons
And what it will take
The choice is awesome
The opportunity is great,
Not knowing what I don't know
Nor what to anticipate

But I know God is with me each step that I take
He said He'd never leave me and never forsake
And the prayer He has answered is for me to take

So, here's to the door He has opened for me
As I embark on this unknown journey
Holding on to Him as tight as I must
Here's to a leap of faith

NIGHTMARE!

It was such a long time ago,
But it seems like yesterday
When you took advantage of her innocent body.
You forced your hands where no one's should have been
And felt what you should not have felt.
You made her see what young eyes should never see
And do what a child should not do.

Feeling cheap, robbed, and dirty,
It was harder to stand strong and say no.
Fighting your strength against hers,
Fragile she was at the time,
Made it ever so harder to release from your grip,
You would not let her go.

She would always struggle
But to no avail.
Your strength was no match for her.
So, tired and breathless as she was from the fight,
She had no choice but to let it be
And wait for your release.

You'd catch her time after time
Wait and grab her, like it was a game.
It made no sense to scream or cry.
You loved her- so you said
With your words,
But she couldn't tell.
You gave her whatever material thing she wanted.

She thought that was love.
She knows better now,
But at the time, her young mind
-like a child who quickly forgives an enemy
Tried to get over what you did,
All for what she thought was love.

And now she's left with these scars and shame
That they say she should not feel.
But even today, the memory is real,
So what is she to do?
She moves on and lives her life.
Each day becomes more bearable than the last
As she remembers her past.

Though the memories remain, she's stronger now.
And the hurt fades a little every day.
Now she knows she should have been treated better.
Because love is pure and unperverted
So, you could not have loved her that way.

GOD

Be Still

Holding on to the promises You gave me
When I want to let go
I remember You made me- and You don't make trash
You said if I needed anything, I could ask

The Creator of all that is, will be, and ever was
God, there's nothing You can't do!
When my life seems small and insignificant
I remember it is big enough for You
And I hold on to what You've told me
When life is kind and doesn't care to know me and tries to throw me away
I remember what You say

Your Word has power to make dry bones rise
So save me from my own demise
And when the tears blind my eyes and heaviness crushes my soul
Lord, help me to just *Be Still and Know.*

THRIVE

I push to function even though I cry
Say I'm okay, though sometimes that's a lie
Put one step in front of the other, 'cause that's what I do
Quitting is a choice I won't choose
        And you wouldn't know the thoughts inside my head
        Some things are better left unsaid
The intensity of feelings can be so consuming
I know God is trying to work through me
But still evil tries to prevail
And wants to see me fail
I've made it this far without losing
Quitting is never a choice I'm choosing
        So, I remember, despite the thoughts inside my head
        Still, some things need not be said
Because He's given me another moment to be alive
Another breath to breathe, another day to survive
And as long as He does, I will always fight
To not only live, but to thrive

He Understands

God promises His love will never fail.
He sees the intent in our plans.
He steadies our steps with His hands
And guides us as we walk toward His promises.

While man looks on the outside,
God sees our hearts
And knows what we need before we say.
We never have to explain to Him.
We can run to Him like a humble child,
And He will shelter us to safety.
Only He satisfies.
When others cannot understand our journey,
He reaches to our soul
And restores what has been torn.

What a comfort it is to have
A God who is our Father and Friend,
Who supplies the needs we don't know we have
And answers us before we ask.
Who understands *everything*
And *is* everything
And is *more* than everything.

Don't Forget Me

Anxiety in life tries to disturb within.
There are periods of peace; then the hustle starts again.
There are no guarantees of safety and sanity of mind,
So where do you go for answers?

God calms when you're under pressure
And heals where there are wounds.
He pacifies when there is conflict and despair.
He's hope when hope eludes.

You may not know the answers,
The how's, the why's, the when's.
But with Him by your side,
You will triumph in the end.

Others may not understand
But that cannot slow you down.
You don't need their understanding
As long as God is around.

There are things you must work through,
But God says, "Don't forget me.
You're searching for peace and healing
And forgetting it comes from Me."

"I'm your source of wisdom;
Your hope, your joy, your guiding light.
I have the answers you seek.
I will always steer you right."

"Don't hesitate to call Me.
I'll be there before you ask.
And don't let your mistakes stop you.
Leave them all in the past."

"You want peace? It's yours.
Let me give you rest.
I'll fight your battles for you.
I'll gladly give you rest."

"Count your blessings, not your sorrows,
For in them you will win.
Don't worry; it won't be long
Until the battles end."

Midnight

Written in 2007

Lying here- my rest interrupted
Sleep put on pause
A "perfect peace" has been made imperfect
As now the silence talks
My eyes are shut, trying to silence the sound
But all I can do is toss and turn round and round ...
Then the tears begin to flow as they often do
My sobs shake me, but I want to lie still
I smother my face in my pillow because
I cannot stand the sound of my own cry
I don't have to look at the clock to know that it's
Midnight

Midnight comes many nights and stays for many days
Carrying with it a loud silence full of thoughts too heavy to say . .
.
-So they force their way through my cry
Though my eyes try to barricade, it is more painful to explain
Than to sit and cry
But the darkness of midnight can see through my eyes
Midnight feels like a place of desolation
Where my cry hits the wall and returns void of consolation
Where the cold sting of the air, in comparison, seems warm

Lying here- alone!
Yet knowing that I am not
He said He would never leave me nor forsake me

So I hold Him to His Word
I let God catch my tears
And as I lift my cry to heaven, my tears return as ammunition
To fight through my brokenness
No longer do I feel the sting of the coldness
Weeping has endured for the night
But joy is on its way
God holds my heart as I pray
And I'm comforted in knowing that He *hears* me!
The perfect peace that I once knew is restored
And as I let Him comfort me
The silence quiets
The tears subside
And He conquers the darkness of midnight

BLACKNESS

I AM BLACK, I AM COMELY

I am black
I am comely

And I am not defined
By the length of my hair, the size that I wear,
Nor the shape of my nose or face

I am not defined
By the size of my thighs, or color of my eyes
Nor my race

I am not defined
By the hue of my skin, or the house I live in,
Nor the car that I drive

I am not defined
By any stereotypes, you have in your mind!

Big-breasted, flat-chested or in between
My beauty is measured by more than you see

So, don't judge me by your self-righteously critical, and superficial definitions
Because I'm more than what you see on the surface.

Instead, see me for my will to walk with my head held high
Or the fact I persevere and never lose my drive

See me for my strength that refuses to let me quit
Or how I believe that true beauty is found by looking within

See me for my determination to fight and never give in
And by my grace to keep my tongue; my restraint to "hold it in."

And before you think again to size me by any ignorant and shallow standards, Hush your mouth and look in your own mirror!

Don't Be a Negro!

Don't be a Negro
Foolish man!
You sow your oats all over town
And then don't care to come around and raise the seed you've sown
You make the home a broken place
And break the promises you make
You kill your wife and child

Don't be a Negro
Foolish man!
You wear your pants below your knees
Your feet are quick to do the deeds that keep you locked away
You waste your time out on street corners
Making it unsafe for your children and brothers
You rape your young black daughters

Don't be a Negro
Foolish man!
You throw sound judgement to the wind; it returns to slap you in the face
But you know not the difference
You sell yourself and waste your time
You let the world leave you behind

Don't be a Negro
Foolish man!

You fall to the lies that the world wants you to believe,
That you can do no better and you shouldn't dream
You give up trying to make for yourself a good name
Too caught up in the wrong influences

Don't be a Negro
Foolish man!
Truly God has called you to be much more than you see
So walk in His path for you
And don't be a Negro-
Be a strong, black, godly man!

LOVE

Hearts of War

I think of you; I have for a while.
But when I see you, I try not to smile.
I cannot give my time nor for too long speak.
I don't want to seem desperate or weak.
So, I put on this façade pretending that I am preoccupied.
When you look for me, I cannot be around.
I cannot show what's really inside.
But it's all a lie; to myself and to you
And my heart deep inside is torn into two.
Like I said, I pretend. But does it work?
I only succeed in hurting us both.
Hearts of war-
It's one heart, yet two
Because my heart is battling
Between loving and not loving you.

Not Yet

The harder I try, the more I realize
That I'm just not ready to let go.
I can speak for today, but tomorrow will arise
Carrying with it a mind of its own.
Though undecided, I might seem
Tomorrow brings its own decisions.
The future can run a choice of its own.
My dreams, though dim, have not died
Though sometimes I feel like a fool
For desiring the thing that I pushed away
What I thought I needed in you.

I feel like a liar to myself,
Especially on hard days
Yet, I know I need time to grieve
And let healing have its way.

So I'm left with this pain that will not go
And chokes me in my throat
As the harder, I try the more I realize
There's one more day
That I cannot say good-bye.

A Broken Love

Moments of frustration
Fiery rage
Anger that could burn a hole into the air
-yet I hold it in
This is how I guessed it could've been
Though I had hoped not
The funniest thing about the matter, though not funny at all
Is despite how much I try, you still cannot see.
It's like the struggle has no answer and the fight has no end.
I won't cry! I shouldn't have denied it could come to this.
So why am I still holding on?
Why can't I let go?
What is holding me where I am?
Nothing!

So, I guess now I'll let go. Good-bye.

After All

We set out focused
On what we thought was ours
And worked to obtain what we just *knew* we had
And as passion burned and desire flamed
We were set!
Cause we just knew it was meant to be.
But later, rather than sooner
And to our dismay
We learned that what we thought was ours
Isn't ours today
And our passion-
Now smothered and left to die
Like a candle once lit but has now lost its flame
Sunken- we ask, "why?"
We knew not then
But now realize that what we thought we had
We saw with blinded eyes
And limited ourselves to only what we saw
Thus, setting us up to fall.
And as the passion burned and desire flamed
We *saw* with our *feelings*
And *felt* with our *eyes*
And so now we move with reservation-
If we even move at all
Because what we thought was sure to be
Turned out *not* to be
After all

Come and Watch the Moon with Me

Come and watch the moon with me
The starry night, the midnight skies
The quiet air beneath me lies
The moonlight dazzles in my eyes
Come see what I see

Come let us watch the sunrise
The flowers praying now open to bloom,
The sun kisses away the moon
As its bright happiness shines to grace the day
Come help me chase the moon away

Come let us catch the skies
And dance the dance of butterflies
In the field of lilies and daffodils
Where peace and happiness abide
Come join me only if you will

Come and look into my eyes
And see the sun outshine the night
And kiss goodbye the midnight moon
And as you look into my eyes
Come see the wilted flower bloom

Come with me to watch the moon!

I'll Leave the Door Ajar for You

I'll leave the door ajar for you
When summer's heat becomes too hot
And you begin to faint
Come find me- and I'll be your shade

I'll leave the door ajar for you
When autumn's leaves change their colors
And love seems to follow others
I'll be there to love you

I'll leave the door ajar for you
In case you need a place to go
When winter's night leaves you cold
I'll keep a space beside me warm

I'll leave the door ajar for you
When springtime greets the world anew
And it seems that no one's there for you
-I'll be

Will you leave the door ajar for me?

In His Arms

In his arms, I dream to be
Pondering as he holds me
I'd press my cheek against his neck
And giggle as he'd kiss my face
As in his arms, I'd rest

In his arms, I dream to be
Pondering as he holds me
He'd gently squeeze above my hips
And kiss my forehead with his lips
As in his arms, I'd sit

In his arms, I dream to be
Pondering as he holds me
I'll press my face against his chest
And lay upon his manly breast
As in his arms, I'd lay

In his arms, I dream to be
Pondering as he holds me
And as we'd gaze up at the stars
The time would never go away
As in his arms, I'd stay

In his arms, I dream to be
Pondering as he holds me
I'll listen to our happy hearts
Beating the rhythm of lovers' hearts
As in his arms, I'll be

Oh, how he holds me!

No More!

No more tears!
Why cry over you?
I'll redirect my passions
And restructure my thoughts
I'll refocus my thinking
And sort out my mind
If I'm not in your thoughts
Why should you be in mine?
I won't waste my tears
I have better things to do
I don't want you to hold me
I don't want to be loved by you
It's just way too complicated
I don't understand
I'd rather not be loved at all
Than be half-loved by a man!

One Million Ways

One million hugs and gentle caresses
One million smiles and loving glances
One million dances in the starlight splendor
One million kisses ever so tender
One million laughs and joys we share
One million ways to say we care

One million times, our eyes meet and lock
One million ways our hearts join and knock
One million sighs of sheer contentment
One million prayers of highest sentiment
One million laughs and joys we share
One million ways to say we care

When I Look into Your Eyes

When I look into your eyes
I see those things your heart says to me
I hear the words your lips don't speak
The things resting in the reservoirs of your soul
Hidden in the deepest places where only my heart can go

And I don't have to ask if you love me
'Cause when I look into your eyes,
        I already know!

When I look into your eyes
I see the love we have today
And all the love we'll have tomorrow
I see you conquer my sorrow
With the weapons of tenderness and purity

And I don't have to doubt your love for me
'Cause when I look into your eyes,
        I believe!

When I look into your eyes
My heart reveals it's all to you
Yet, we do not have to say a word
Our silence speaks loud enough for us to hear
The secrets tucked away- there's nothing we cannot say

And I don't have to guard my words
'Cause when I look into your eyes,
        I know I'm heard!

When I look into your eyes
I trust those things I see
Powerful signals you convey- your eyes don't lie to me
All the things you say, my eyes say back to you

And I don't have to fear the truth
'Cause when I look into your eyes
I know it's really you!

Convicted

Living in the dream of what will never come to be
Now I know this is not what God wants for me
But how do I get out?

At times I feel that this is too much
And I'm better off giving up
-on everything-
But I know God has much more for me.

Tired of living a lie
And pretending to be happy
Not sure which steps to take
Have I already gotten in the way of
What the future has for me?

Sometimes I want to know, "God, what's next?"
"You already know what I'm going to do
So let me know too.
Maybe then I won't' be disappointed."

But now, with conviction, I move
The path is clear; the steps marked
I ask God to hold my hand and walk me through the windy road
That is often lonely and dark.

God's promises hold me, and He is my Comforter
When deeper and deeper the pain becomes
The faster to Him I run

-only He can heal within.

The race is not given to the swift but to those who don't quit
Trusting in God, I'm believing that His power will see me through
And He will keep me nigh to Him
-This, my God can do!

Just Yesterday

Just yesterday
I saw your face and caught your pretty smile
And it was then that I knew that I wanted to know you more
But I made no attempt to meet you
I just watched you from afar.

Just yesterday
We parted ways
If only I'd known-
You said goodbye without ever saying hello to a man you'd never known
I thought you'd walked out and that maybe this was "it."
The love had ended before it even had the chance to begin
So, sadly, I left.
But thoughts of you lingered in my mind.

Just yesterday
I reached home- hundreds of miles away- and got up the nerve to send you a message
Was this weird? Or maybe even awkward?
I truly did not want to make you uncomfortable.
But you wrote back!
And we wrote back and forth.
All was good and then…

Just yesterday
I gave you a call, and for the first time, we spoke.

To hear your voice meant so much to me
I still remember the words we said.
I'd prayed every time I wrote or spoke to you
For everything to be just right
And before I knew it,

It was
Just yesterday
That I crossed the border and drove three hours
Just to hold you in my arms
I couldn't help but wonder if it was real.
Maybe it was just an illusion.
Nevertheless, we were together.
And the moments we shared were so special
If only they had never ended.

Just yesterday
My life changed so drastically
I met this girl and fell in love
And today, she loves me in return
Yesterday was such a long day.

How Long is Forever?

How long is forever and who says so?
"Always and forever"
"Til death do us part"
"Best friends forever"
"until eternity."

Well, if death can do us part
Then forever has an end
And if we're "best friends forever" today
And worst enemies tomorrow,
Then who is to say that there even is an eternity?

"Time will tell"
Is an old cliché
But even time can cease and leave us premature.
If I put my faith in your words, will they be strong enough to hold me?
And if I trust in your promises,
Will they be certain to carry me to the time of their promised fulfillment?

How long is forever?
And how long should it be?
Will today's "forever" reach tomorrow's?
And will tomorrow's reach eternity?

Love My Hurt Away

You told me you love me
You said I have your heart
You said you'd always be there for me
Even when we're apart
You told me not to shut down
Or push you away
If everything is still alright
Then why do I feel this way?
    Why can't I stop the tears?
    Why am I not okay?
    Why do I feel so lonely?
    Why does it hurt this way?
I just want you to hold me
And let me feel your strength
I need someone to understand
That I don't want to feel like this
I don't like the fear of the unknown
The future I cannot see
I need you to show me that you'll still be there
And you'll always love me
    Please help me stop the tears
    Please help me to be okay
    Please help me not feel lonely
    Please love my hurt away

For Now

For Now
We sit here
Glancing into each other's eyes
What is it that we feel?
I squeeze your hand, and you squeeze mine
I laugh without always knowing why
Can't explain how you make me feel

For Now
I always think of you
And know you do the same
Man, what is it about you?
Could sit and talk for hours…
Which is just what we do-
And then turn around and do it again the next day
Funny how we are this way

For Now
Comfortable, yet nervous
Free, yet reserved
Calm, yet excited
Conflicting emotions juxtapose themselves
As if playing a tug-of-war
And each time I see you
I feel something more

For Now
Just letting things be, what they are- what they will
Can't rush destiny

Not confined to a title, or even a box of time
You say I'm yours- I pray you're mine
And hope this love is not blind
As with caution and patience, we move

And as I sit here with you and sweetly ponder
I hope and pray deep within my heart
That this is real
And that I would know with certainty
That someway, somehow
I'll always have you -For Now

DEDICATIONS

A Virtuous Mother

Proverbs 31:10

"Who can find a virtuous woman?
Her worth is far above rubies?

She sacrifices her own desires
And provides her children's needs
She quickly answers their cry for help
While never counting the cost

She clothes herself with respect and integrity
For she knows that her children have eyes . . .
And ears, and mouths, and feet and hands
That mimic what she does

She moves cautiously in the dark
Knowing that the light exposes her true character
And she's not too proud to pass along
The hard lessons she's had to learn

She honor's God outside the home
By instilling in her children honesty and morals
Her children know
How to treat their fellow man

She honors God inside the home
By teaching her children to love and respect themselves and each other
Her sons know that love is not abusive or disrespectful towards their mother

And her daughters know that love is not the embodiment
Of everyone who calls himself "Man"

She instructs her children in the things of God
Her children are trained in obedience
And they grow in wisdom and in stature
As they learn to obey the voice of God

Who can find a virtuous Mother?
Her worth is far above rubies

You Deserve More

Written for my mother, Denise D. VanNess for Mother's Day 2002

You deserve more
For becoming a mother before your time
By raising your siblings and then your own
Many times with the help of God alone
For living your life when it seemed easier not to
While constantly fighting battles within and without
And then winning the fight over cancer

You deserve more
For putting up with broken relationships,
Shattered dreams and empty promises
By people who were important in your life . . .
Or at least you thought they were

You deserve more
And only God knows how
Sadly though, as you have been shown
It may not just come to you
Sure, you've had some rainbows after the clouds
And some smiles after the tears
But only God knows just what you had to endure
To *find* the rainbow and *hold* the smile

You deserve more
So why not be a little gentler on yourself?
And a little easier on others?
You deserve only the best out of life
So why not go get it?

It's yours!
You've waited long enough!

Beautifully Strong!

Written for Alexus in 2009

Beautifully strong!
That's who you are inside and out
A one-of-a kind spirit God has given you
To carry you far beyond your highest doubts
Amazing strength He has endowed within you to free your own soul
But do you even know just how much strength you hold?

Your strength is in the song you sing with your voice
So elegantly and sweetly as a heavenly bird
And the song you sing so passionately and fierce-
Commanding that your soul be heard

Your strength is in the story that you tell
With your pencil and paint in hand
Bright colors, or dark and gray
Your art brings to life what your heart wants to say

Your strength is in your bubbly joy
Infectious to all who come around
Rubbing off indiscriminately
To cure their broken smiles

Having said all this, my dear sister,
Now, do you see the strength you have inside?

Indeed, it is this same strength that carries you

When life can be unkind

This same strength keeps you tall
When life comes to knock you down

This same strength that helps you swim
When you feel you're about to drown

So keep singing
Keep shining
Keep drawing
Keep smiling
Keep pushing your way as high as you want to be

And through it all
May you always remain
Beautifully Strong!

My Sweet Child

-Dedicated to my sons Grayson and Braylon

My sweet child
God gave to me
To love and nurture unconditionally
To teach the ways of life and more
To help you grow, and watch you explore

My sweet child
It amazes me
With how you learn and love, and adapt
You see the world with innocent eyes
Enrapt in the wonders of life

My sweet child
So precious and kind
You give with your heart; you open your mind
To possibilities before you
I'm blessed to call you mine

My sweet child
It makes me afraid
To know this life will bring you pain
and break your precious heart
To know you will one day grow and open your eyes
To the many things that are ugly and hard

My sweet child
Please never forget you're in God's hands
You may have dreams, but He has bigger plans

And He will always steer you right
Let Him be your guiding light

My sweet child
Please keep your heart
Please keep your smile
Please keep your joy
Please never lose who you are!

THANK YOU!

For My Husband Chrys
(June 8, 2009)

For encouraging me and not letting me give up on myself
For being gentle when telling me the truth, and never judging or criticizing me
For accepting my "weirdness" and letting me be silly
For lifting me high when I'm feeling low
For being proud of me and letting everyone know just how much you are
For being open about your faults and forgiving me for mine
For being my biggest supporter and cheerleader from day one-like you said you would
For telling me that I'm worth it and dispelling any of my doubts that I'm not
For hiding encouraging notes around my house-so I could smile days and weeks later
For telling me every single day that I am gorgeous and intelligent-and that you love me
For being there and being present
For paying attention to the little things and the smallest details
For always making me laugh- even when I don't want to and for allowing me to feel safe with you
For the time you sat on the floor by my bedside until I fell asleep-all so I wouldn't have to cry alone
For believing in me those times I couldn't see the worth in myself
For loving me past my pain
For being my friend, my lover, and my husband
For all these things and more, Christopher Herring-I thank you!

Dear Me

Words of affirmation I wrote for myself

Remember when you thought
You wouldn't make it?
Remember when You thought
You would quit?
Well, look how far you've come!
Life's not a rush, so take your time.
You're doing just fine.
It will work out. It always has.
The darkest night will come to pass
Into the brightest day.
You really are okay.
The lessons you've learned along the way
And trials you've had to face
They did not discriminate because of your young age.
They've made you who you are today.
And yet you are not done!
A wife, a mother, a sister, a friend…
Tomorrow you'll be a better one.
And while you journey to tomorrow
Appreciate who you are today.
Give yourself your own applause
Because, here's the thing,
Each day that you awake, you've already made it!

ABOUT THE AUTHOR

TaNaasha (Ta-Nay-sha) Herring is an active Christian, mom of two little boys, and wife who has enjoyed music, reading, and fitness from a young age. She holds a Bachelor of Arts degree in Sociology and a Bachelor of Science degree in Nursing. She has been a nurse since 2008 and plans to continue working in this capacity to empower and educate others on how to care for themselves on a functional and wholistic level.

To reach the author, please contact her via email at strings4heaven@gmail.com, her Facebook page https://facebook.com/tanaasha.herring
Or IG page: https://instagram.com/its_ta_nay_sha

For book purchases please contact author through PayPal or Payhip:

www.paypal.me/TaNaashaBHerring

www.payhip.com/TBHerringBooks

His Glory Creations Publishing, LLC is an International Christian Book Publishing Company, which helps launch the creative fiction and non-fiction works of new, aspiring and seasoned authors across the globe, through stories that are inspirational, empowering, life-changing or educational in nature, including poetry, journals, children's books, and recipe books.

DESIRE TO KNOW MORE?

<u>Contact Information:</u>

CEO/Founder: Felicia C. Lucas

www.hisglorycreationspublishing.com

Email: hgcpublishingllc@gmail.com

Phone: 919-679-1706

Made in the USA
Middletown, DE
26 February 2023

25372404R00056